Contents

Introduction

What's it like in the polar regions?

Do you like ice cubes in your drinks? Think how your hand feels as you take them from the freezer. It goes from the temperature of the kitchen (about 20°C) to −10°C inside the freezer. Do you think it would be colder if you lived near one of the Poles and you put your hand outside your door? The answer is a definite yes – and if the polar winds were blowing, they would make it feel even colder. If you stood outside in your everyday clothes, you would not survive for long. Even in summer the temperature may only rise to about 0°C. That is the temperature of the ice cubes you put in your drink.

The keys to survival

There are two polar regions: the Arctic, around the North Pole, and the Antarctic, around the South Pole. The Arctic is an area of ocean, covered in ice and surrounded by land. The Antarctic is a huge, ice-covered landmass.

Thousands of years ago people moved into the Arctic lands and learned to survive there. But conditions in the Antarctic were too harsh for people to set up home. In the twentieth century scientists set up **research stations** in the Arctic and the Antarctic, which are still in use today. Scientists go to study the weather, the rocks and the living things that survive in the polar regions. But first they plan how they will survive, thinking for example about clothing, travel, shelter, and staying healthy in the cold and ice and snow.

▶ *This research scientist in the Antarctic will drive the small vehicle called a snowmobile, to pull the sledge loaded with equipment.*

Discovering with science

For thousands of years people have investigated their surroundings and made discoveries that have helped them survive. About 400 years ago, a way of investigating called the scientific method was devised, to help us understand our world more clearly. The main features of the scientific method are:

1 Making an **observation**

2 Thinking of an idea to explain the observation

3 Doing a test or experiment to test the idea

4 Looking at the result of the test and comparing it with the idea

Today the scientific method is used to provide explanations for almost everything. In this book you can find out about the science that helps people, plants and animals survive in the polar regions. You can also try some activities to see how different areas of science, such as materials and light, help life survive in the coldest places on Earth. In these activities you may use the whole of the scientific method or just parts of it, such as making observations or doing experiments. But you will always be using science to make discoveries.

Are you ready to find out how people survive in the polar regions? Turn the page to find out about these regions of the Earth.

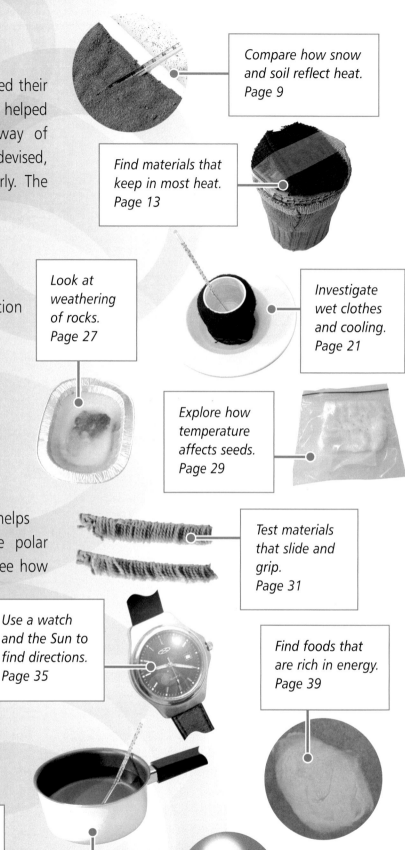

Compare how snow and soil reflect heat.
Page 9

Find materials that keep in most heat.
Page 13

Look at weathering of rocks.
Page 27

Investigate wet clothes and cooling.
Page 21

Explore how temperature affects seeds.
Page 29

Test materials that slide and grip.
Page 31

Use a watch and the Sun to find directions.
Page 35

Find foods that are rich in energy.
Page 39

Investigate how size affects heat loss.
Page 43

Use light to send signals.
Page 45

The polar regions

The Earth spins in space, around its **axis** – an imaginary line through the centre of the planet. It does not spin in an upright position, but is tipped to one side.

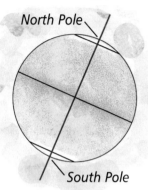

North Pole

South Pole

The places where the ends of the axis meet the surface of the Earth are the Poles. The region around the North Pole is the Arctic, and the region around the South Pole is the Antarctic.

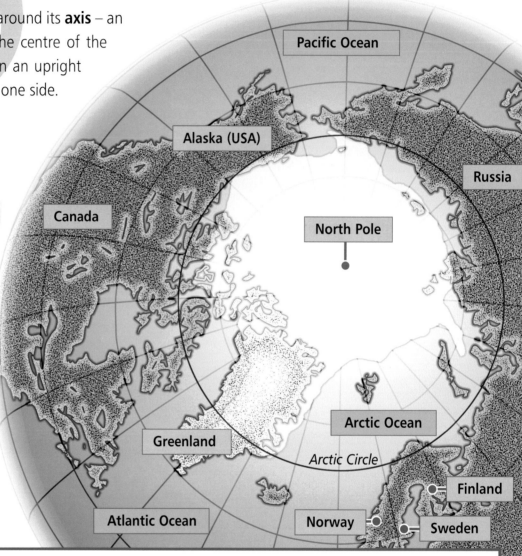

Pacific Ocean

Alaska (USA)

Russia

Canada

North Pole

Greenland

Arctic Ocean

Arctic Circle

Finland

Atlantic Ocean

Norway

Sweden

The Arctic

The North Pole is near the middle of a huge sheet of ice that floats in the Arctic Ocean. The map shows the size of the ice sheet in summer. In winter, more of the ocean freezes over and the ice sheet reaches many of the surrounding coasts.

The Inuit people live in Greenland, Canada, Alaska (USA) and on the northeast coast of Russia. The Sami people live in Norway, Sweden, Finland and parts of

Russia. The area in which they live is also known as Lapland. Other small groups of people, such as the Chukchi, live in the northern parts of Russia. All the places where people live are hundreds of kilometres away from the North Pole.

There are two parts to the Arctic: the ice sheet and the land around the Arctic Ocean called the **tundra,** *where* **lichens**, *grasses and small plants grow. Animals include arctic foxes, polar bears and snowy owls.*

The Antarctic

The South Pole is found on land that is covered with ice. The land called the continent of Antarctica covers 14 million square kilometres. That is almost twice the size of the continent of Australia.

The map shows Antarctica in the summer. In winter, ice develops all round the coast and spreads out millions of square kilometres in all directions.

The Antarctic was not discovered until explorers were able to make long expeditions across the seas. James Cook sailed round Antarctica in the eighteenth century and saw many seals and whales. When people learned of this, settlements were set up so the seals and whales could be hunted. These are not used for hunting today, but there are many research stations in which scientists live and work.

Penguins live in this ice-covered land. There are very few plants – mostly lichens and mosses.

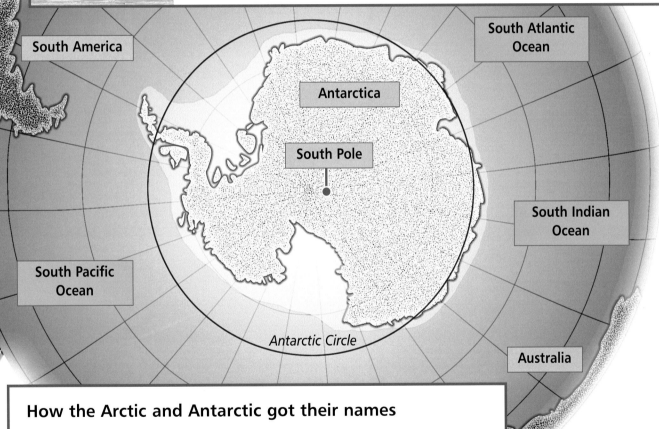

South America

South Atlantic Ocean

Antarctica

South Pole

South Indian Ocean

South Pacific Ocean

Australia

Antarctic Circle

How the Arctic and Antarctic got their names

Expeditions to the Arctic began in the times of the ancient Greeks, and it was the Greeks who gave both regions their names. They noticed that a **constellation** of stars appeared to turn round over the North Pole region. They thought the constellation looked like a bear ('arctos' in Greek) and so they named the region the Arctic. Today we usually call this constellation the Plough, Great Bear or Big Dipper.

The ancient Greeks believed that the world was an orderly place. They reasoned that, since there is an Arctic region, there must also be an 'Antarctic' region in a place opposite to the Arctic. They never visited the Antarctic.

Why the polar regions are so cold

The curve of the Earth's surface

The surface of the Earth receives heat from the Sun. Different parts of the Earth receive different amounts of heat because of the way its surface curves away from the Sun. At the equator the surface curves only slightly away from the Sun. This means that a sunbeam striking the Earth at the equator covers just a small area of the surface. The heat rays in the beam are close together and heat the surface strongly.

In the polar regions the surface of the Earth curves away greatly from the Sun. A sunbeam that strikes the Earth at one of the Poles is more spread out than one that strikes at the equator. The heat rays in the beam have more surface to heat, and so they heat it less strongly.

Reflecting heat

Rays of heat can be **reflected**, just like rays of light. The reflective power of a surface is called the **albedo**. The white surfaces of snow in the polar regions have a high albedo. This means that a large amount of the heat that reaches the snow is reflected back into space. This loss of heat is another factor that makes the polar regions cold.

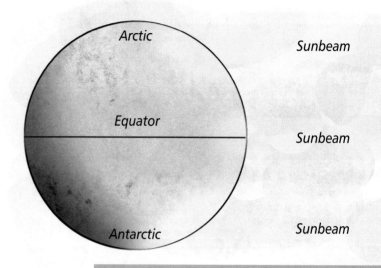

In the polar regions, the surface of the Earth curves away from the Sun. The rays in a sunbeam cover a much greater area than at the equator.

This photograph taken from space of part of Antarctica shows how the white surface reflects light and heat.

Comparing the reflection of heat

Does snow reflect more heat than soil? In this investigation, white card is used to represent snow and black card is used to represent soil. You can use heat rays from the Sun or from a light bulb to test the albedos of 'snow' and 'soil'.

You need two small polystyrene trays, scissors, a spoon, sand, two thermometers, black card, white card.

1 Cut a notch in one long side of each tray. Then spoon sand into each tray, up to the notch.

2 Rest a thermometer in the notch and on the sand in each tray. Then fill each tray with sand up to the rim.

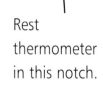

Rest thermometer in this notch.

3 Cover one tray with white card and the other with black card. Read the thermometers and record the temperature of the sand in the two trays.

Add more sand to fill to the rim.

4 Leave the trays in the Sun or under a table lamp for half an hour. Then read and record the temperatures again.

5 Compare the temperature change of the sand beneath 'snow' with the temperature change of the sand beneath 'soil'. You should find that the sand under the black card has warmed up more than the sand under the white card.

Weather conditions in the polar regions

Polar travellers must take shelter in a blizzard. Afterwards they will need to dig the tents out of the snow.

Why does it snow?

Snow is made from crystals of ice. It forms in the following way. There is a gas called **water vapour** in the air. As it rises in the air, it meets cooler and cooler temperatures and eventually **condenses** on dust particles, making tiny water droplets. The huge numbers of water droplets form clouds. At the top of the cloud, where the temperature is 0°C, the water droplets freeze together and form ice crystals.

The ice crystals are much larger and heavier than the water droplets in the cloud and start to fall towards the ground. As they fall, they may move into slightly warmer air. This makes them melt a little and they become stuck together, forming quite large snowflakes. This type of snow is common in the winter in many countries that are not near the Poles.

At the Poles, the air below the snow clouds is so cold that the crystals do not form large flakes. They form small flakes, which means that the snow that falls is powdery.

Blizzards

It is often windy in the polar regions. A strong wind can sweep the powdery snow into the air and make a blizzard. Very little can be seen because the snowflakes fill the air. When a wind whips up a blizzard, explorers must set up their tents and shelter until the wind drops and the snow settles again.

The danger of ultraviolet light

Ultraviolet light is present in sunbeams. It is harmful to all life. We cannot see it, but it affects our bodies by causing sunburn. Large amounts of ultraviolet light can cause skin cancers.

Whenever sunlight and lightning pass through the air, they change some of the oxygen in the air into another gas called ozone. This collects in a layer about 25 kilometres above the Earth, higher than the air that can be blown about by winds. The ozone layer prevents large amounts of ultraviolet light reaching the Earth's surface. However, in some places the ozone layer has been damaged.

Some gases called **CFCs** have been made for use in aerosols and in the machines that make fridges cool. It was discovered that when an aerosol was sprayed or an old fridge was broken up, the CFCs escaped into the atmosphere and destroyed some of the ozone in the ozone layer. Today other gases such as carbon dioxide, which do not destroy ozone, are used instead of CFCs. But there are still large amounts of CFCs in the atmosphere, which attack the ozone.

At the Poles, the unusual weather conditions of a very long, cold winter followed by a short, warm summer cause the CFCs to destroy large amounts of ozone when the air warms up. This makes holes in the ozone layer above the Poles each spring. They remain there throughout the warmer weather. Ultraviolet light can then stream through the holes. People living in the polar regions cover most of their bodies to keep warm, but they must also protect their faces with special creams to prevent skin damage.

This scientist at a research station in the Antarctic is releasing a weather balloon, which will take measurements of ozone in the atmosphere.

Clothes for the polar regions

Hypothermia

Hypothermia is a condition that occurs when the temperature inside the body falls below its natural, healthy temperature of 37°C. When the temperature falls below this, the person starts to think and move more slowly, and may have spasms of shivering and headaches. A further drop in the body temperature can lead to unconsciousness and death.

Hypothermia can be caused by standing in a strong, cold wind or falling into cold water. It is treated by removing the source of the coldness – for example, moving the person out of the wind or changing them into dry clothes. They should be given a warm drink, if they are conscious, and then put in a warm sleeping bag.

Frostbite

If the skin and flesh beneath it fall to a temperature of −1°C, they freeze and frostbite occurs. A person beginning to suffer from frostbite may feel a prickling sensation in the skin. The skin may then look waxy and feel numb, before it becomes sore and forms blisters. The ears, nose, face, hands and feet are most in danger of becoming frostbitten because they may be exposed to the cold conditions. Frostbite can be cured, if it is not too severe, by warming up the affected part of the body. If a finger or toe is very badly damaged by frostbite, it may simply fall off.

This Antarctic scientist has covered her face entirely, to avoid frostbite.

Which material keeps in most heat?

Heat always moves from a warm place to a cooler place. In polar conditions, clothes must stop heat from escaping from your warm body into the cold air. In this activity, you compare how different materials stop heat passing through them – or keep in the heat. This kind of investigation is made by scientists selecting materials for making clothes for polar regions.

You need plastic cups, cardboard, materials (e.g. wool, silk, cotton, nylon), scissors, sticky tape, warm water, a thermometer, a stop clock.

1 Make a cardboard lid for each plastic cup.

2 Cut pieces of one material, to cover one cup and its lid completely. Tape the material in place.

3 Cover each cup and lid with a different material, in exactly the same way.

4 Almost fill the first cup with warm water (about 50°C). Take the temperature of the water, then put on the lid. Write down the temperature.

5 Repeat step 4 with the other cups.

6 Take the temperature of the water in the cups every 5 minutes for 30 minutes and write down each one.

7 Look at how the temperature of the water fell in each cup. In which cup did it fall the least? The material around that cup keeps in the most heat.

Side piece

Base

Lid

Tape one piece of material to lid.

Wrap material around the cup.

Measure temperature every 5 minutes.

Tape a piece of the same material to the base of the cup.

Using air to keep warm

Air is a very poor **conductor** of heat. This means that heat cannot pass through it easily. Many polar clothes are designed or worn so that they trap one or more layers of air to help stop heat escaping from the body.

Some clothes, such as body warmers, have padded sections. Air is trapped in the pads. The Inuit used to wear underclothes made from sealskin, with the fur facing inwards. The fur trapped a layer of air to stop the body heat escaping.

*A woollen **balaclava** helps to stop heat escaping from the head and neck. The jacket hood is worn over this. It has drawstrings which allow it to be closed over most of the face, to prevent frostbite and damage from ultraviolet light.*

Polar travellers today wear brightly coloured clothes so that they can be easily seen against the snow and ice.

*Jacket and trousers have a windproof surface so the wind cannot pass inside. Under the surface is a thick **insulating** layer, which may be made of goose down.*

A woollen vest is worn under the jacket, and woollen long johns are worn under the trousers.

Mittens with drawstrings prevent snow entering at the wrist. The mittens are covered in a waterproof material and have a layer of insulating material inside to keep the hands warm. A pair of gloves may be worn under the mittens. These are also made from an insulating material such as wool. If the fingers need to be used to open a food packet or assemble a tent, the mittens can be removed and the woolly gloves will keep the hands warm as they work.

Two or maybe three pairs of socks stop heat escaping from the feet. Boots may be lined with insulating material.

14

The furry hood

Furry hoods are part of the traditional dress of the Inuit and are also worn by polar travellers today. The fur is not for decoration. It has an important purpose. When people breathe out, they release some water vapour into the air from their lungs. The water vapour passes through the fur around the hood and freezes on it. If the fur was not there, the water vapour may freeze on the skin of the face and cause frostbite.

 Traditional Inuit clothes are made from animal skins and fur. Today the Inuit also wear clothes made from modern manmade materials.

Avoiding snow blindness

The white surface of the snow reflects large amounts of light. This can enter the eyes and dazzle them, like bright car headlights. Dazzling light like this is called glare. It makes it difficult to see. Polar travellers wear goggles, which have **lenses** like sunglasses to prevent large numbers of light rays reaching the eyes.

If the eyes are not protected, snow blindness can occur. Everything starts to look pink, then red, and there is pain in the eyes. Think of a time when you had a piece of grit in your eye. Now think how it would feel with 100 pieces of grit and you will have an idea of what snow blindness is like. It is not permanent. It is cured by wearing a blindfold and resting in a dark place.

People who have lost or broken their goggles can avoid snow blindness if they can find some bark. This can be cut into the shape of goggles, with thin horizontal slits in front of each eye, so that only some light rays can pass through.

Summer and winter in the polar regions

The seasons that we have on the Earth are due to the way the Earth travels around the Sun. The Earth takes one year to travel in its **orbit** around the Sun. Remember that the Earth is also spinning round on its axis and that the axis is slightly tilted. As the Earth travels around the Sun, the direction of the tilt always stays the same.

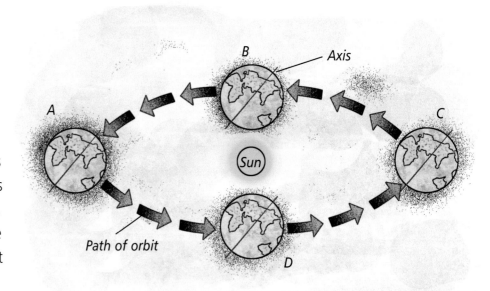

The Earth can be divided into two halves, called the Northern and Southern Hemispheres. When the Northern Hemisphere is tilted towards the Sun (A), it is summer there and winter in the Southern Hemisphere. When the Northern Hemisphere is tilted away from the Sun (C), it is winter there and summer in the Southern Hemisphere. When the Hemispheres are neither tilted towards nor tilted away from the Sun (B and D), there are the seasons called spring and autumn.

As the Earth travels around the Sun, different parts of it face towards or away from the Sun and this gives us the seasons. At position A, for example, it is summer for the Arctic and winter for the Antarctic.

The path of the Sun across the sky

The Earth's orbit around the Sun affects the way the Sun is seen to move across the sky, at any place on the Earth. Near the equator, the Sun appears on the horizon at about 6 o'clock in the morning. It gradually rises very high in the sky and then sinks and sets at about 6 o'clock in the evening.

How the Sun appears to move across the sky at the equator

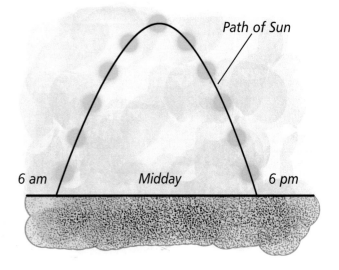

Summertime

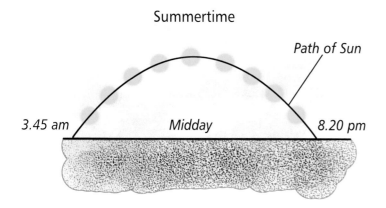

Path of Sun

3.45 am   Midday   8.20 pm

Wintertime

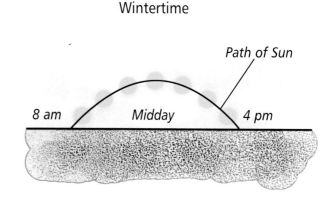

Path of Sun

8 am   Midday   4 pm

In regions north of the equator, such as in the UK and the northern states of the USA, the path of the Sun may vary in the following way. In summer, the Sun appears at about a quarter to four in the morning, rises high in the sky and sets at about twenty past eight in the evening. In winter, the Sun appears on the horizon at about 8 o'clock in the morning, rises only a little way in the sky, and sets at about 4 o'clock in the afternoon.

In regions north of an imaginary line around the Earth called the **Arctic Circle**, something unusual happens in summer. The Sun never sets. In winter in these regions the Sun never rises. At this time the weather is coldest of all. A similar thing happens in regions south of an imaginary line called the **Antarctic Circle**.

The polar regions experience these periods when the Sun never sets or never rises because there are times during the Earth's orbit when these parts of the planet are facing towards or away from the Sun, throughout the day.

These photos of the Sun were taken using a time-lapse process, on a summer day in the Arctic Circle. The camera took six pictures over a period of time. They show how the Sun dips towards the horizon and then begins to rise again. The darkness is due to the light filter on the camera, which allows a picture of the Sun to be taken.

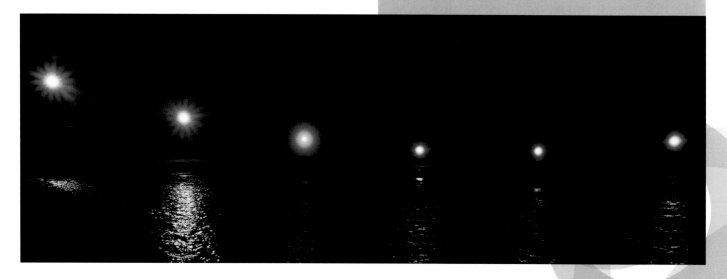

Light and dark at the Poles

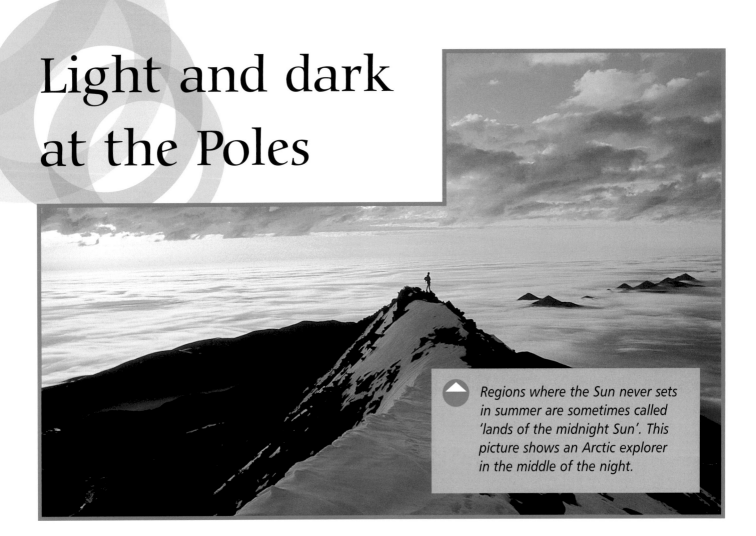

Regions where the Sun never sets in summer are sometimes called 'lands of the midnight Sun'. This picture shows an Arctic explorer in the middle of the night.

In the polar regions, there is a period of three months when the Sun never sets. When this period of continuous sunlight ends, the polar regions are not immediately plunged into darkness. The Sun starts to rise and set as it does at other places on the Earth. Eventually the Sun does not rise at all, but at this time there is twilight in the sky. This is the kind of light we get in the skies before sunrise and after sunset. Eventually, a period of complete darkness occurs in mid-winter, but it only lasts a month before twilight returns to the sky as another summer approaches.

Planning an expedition

People planning an expedition in a polar region take into account how the light changes during the year. They may plan to get to the starting point of the expedition in the twilight, then make their expedition during the time when there is sunlight. Finally, they may plan to complete their expedition before it is too dark to find their way and avoid hazards, such as **crevasses**.

Light and plants

Plants make food for their survival. They need energy to do this and they get this energy from sunlight. In the polar regions in summer, the plants can make large amounts of food from the sunlight. They do not use all the food at once but store it in their stems and roots to use in winter when there is no light to make food (see also page 28).

Coping with the midnight Sun

Most people on the planet are awake during the hours of sunlight and sleep when it is dark. When they visit polar regions in the summer, they find that there is sunlight in the sky day and night. They have to get used to sleeping when it is daylight.

Why do auroras happen in the polar regions?

The Earth behaves as if it contains a large magnet. The magnetic force from this magnet makes compasses on the Earth's surface point north and south. The magnetic force also spreads out into space. The Sun releases billions of tiny particles of matter into space every second. Some of the particles which pass the Earth are attracted by the Earth's magnetic forces and move down into the atmosphere near the Poles, because that is where the strongest magnetic forces occur. As the particles crash into particles of gas high in the atmosphere, sheets of flickering green, yellow or red light are produced. These sheets of light are known as the Aurora Borealis in the Arctic and the Aurora Australis in the Antarctic.

The best displays of aurora lights are seen in winter when the sky is dark. This is the Aurora Borealis. The lights are seen best in the polar regions, but can sometimes be seen in places further away.

SAD

Some people who live in conditions where there are long periods of darkness, like the polar winter, can suffer from SAD. These letters stand for seasonal affective disorder. People who suffer from SAD can have a wide range of symptoms, including feeling tired and miserable, sleeping for long periods and finding it difficult to concentrate. Scientists are still investigating how to help people who suffer from SAD. One treatment used at the moment is for the sufferer to sit in a bright light for up to three-quarters of an hour.

Ice in the Arctic

The North Pole is near the middle of the Arctic Ocean. It is so cold here that the ocean surface has turned to ice. This mass of floating ice is known as pack ice and it can be 4 metres thick. The area covered by the pack ice increases in winter as more of the ocean freezes. At this time the ice reaches all the shores around the edge of the ocean.

When summer approaches, large areas of the pack ice begin to melt. It breaks into huge, flat-topped slabs of ice. This can be a great danger to people on an expedition. They may travel across the ice and come to a gap where the ice has cracked. There is water in the gap, from the ocean below. They must find a small gap, to cross safely. If they jump across, they may slip into the water. They must be pulled out as quickly as possible and change into dry clothes, because wet clothes can make the body cool down very fast.

These scientists in the Arctic are taking samples of blocks of pack ice, to investigate how it formed.

Why ice floats

All substances are made from tiny particles that can only be seen using the most powerful microscopes. If the particles are packed together very closely, the substance is said to have a high **density**. If the particles are packed together less closely, the substance is said to have a lower density, or to be less dense.

 High-density substance

 Low-density substance

A substance that is denser than water sinks in it. A substance that is less dense than water floats. When water turns to ice, it becomes less dense because its particles spread out more. This change in density lets the ice float so that two-sevenths of it sticks out above the water.

Ice

Water

How fast do wet clothes cool down a body?

You are going to make some cold water like that in the gaps in the ice, and then see how fast a sock dipped into this water can cool down a body. The body is a model – a plastic cup full of warm water.

You need woollen socks, ice cubes in some water, two plastic cups, two dishes, two thermometers, clock, warm water (about 50°C maximum).

Cup in wet sock

1 Dip one sock into the ice and water. Keep it in for about 30 seconds.

2 Pull the sock out and let water drip from it back into the container.

3 Put a plastic cup inside the sock and place the sock and cup in a dish, so that any more water leaving the sock can collect there.

Immerse the sock for 30 seconds.

4 Put the second plastic cup inside the dry sock and set it up in the second dish.

5 Almost fill each plastic cup with warm water. Then take the temperature of the water in each cup every minute for 15 minutes. Write down the temperatures as you take them.

Cup in dry sock

6 Compare how the water in the two cups cooled down.

21

From snow to iceberg

When snow settles in the polar regions, very little of it melts. It forms a layer, which gets squashed when more snow falls on top of it. As the snow is squashed, some of the air between the snowflakes is pushed out and a material called **firn** is made. As more snow falls, the firn is squashed even more and more air escapes. This extra squashing turns firn into ice.

The ice forms huge sheets over the land in both polar regions. These sheets are called **ice caps**. The two main ice caps are the Greenland ice cap in the north polar region and the Antarctic ice cap in the south polar region.

Where the ice collects in valleys between mountains, **glaciers** form. As the ice in both sheets and glaciers is formed on high ground, it is gradually pulled down, by the force of gravity, to the level of the sea at the coasts.

During warm weather, glacier ice at the coast begins to melt and break up. The ice splinters as it breaks up and produces irregular-shaped icebergs. When sheet ice reaches the water's edge it may float out on it, forming an **ice shelf**. Eventually, part of the ice shelf melts and the rest breaks up to form flat-topped icebergs. The process of making icebergs is called calving.

In this photograph you can see how the Greenland ice cap and a glacier move towards sea level. In the background are many flat-topped icebergs.

When ice breaks off the end of a glacier, it makes irregular-shaped icebergs.

Icebergs and ships

Icebergs in the Arctic float away to the south and can be a danger to ships. Only two-sevenths of an iceberg appears above the water surface, and its lower part may be much wider than the part that can be seen. If a ship sails close to an iceberg, the part of the iceberg that is under the water can strike the ship's hull. The ice is so hard that it can break through the steel from which the hull is made and make a hole in it. Water can then gush through the hole and sink the ship.

Collisions with icebergs have often occurred in fog. In foggy conditions, the iceberg is not seen until just before the ship hits it. Today, scientists go out and attach a **beacon** to an iceberg floating close to the path of ships. The beacon sends signals to the scientists, which they can use to work out the iceberg's position. This information is passed on to ships' crews, so they can steer their ships away from the iceberg. Maps showing the positions of icebergs are also made to help ships avoid them.

Floating to safety

If people find they cannot finish an expedition and cannot send for help, they may try to use ice to float to a shore or to a place where there may be a chance of them being seen and rescued. This is very dangerous, because the ice may melt before safety is found. Flat ice may be used, because it does not turn over. An iceberg with an irregular shape may turn over as it melts, throwing everyone into the water.

Ice in the Antarctic

In the icy world of the Antarctic, penguins and seals are the only large animals that can survive.

In the Arctic, most of the ice forms on the Greenland ice cap and in the Arctic Ocean. In the Antarctic, most of the ice forms on the land of the Antarctic continent. Also, in the winter, large parts of the Antarctic Ocean freeze over, making pack ice. The ice on the land moves to the coast, in a similar way to the ice in Arctic lands (see page 22).

Ships trapped in ice

The freezing over of the ocean can be a special danger to ships supplying the Antarctic research stations with food and equipment. The ships must leave the ocean before they are trapped in the pack ice. If a ship gets stuck in the pack ice, the ice can squash on its sides and make holes in the ship's hull. When the ice melts and loses its grip on the ship, water can gush through the holes, causing the ship to sink.

Many ships have an ice-breaker attached to the front, so that they can break their way clear if the ice is not too thick.

Crevasses

As a glacier moves along, the movement causes pushing and pulling forces in the ice and this can make huge cracks appear in it. These cracks are called crevasses. They are found in all glaciers but are a particular problem to travellers in the Antarctic, as many routes across the continent are over glaciers. The crevasses can be very deep, so anyone falling to the bottom would be killed instantly. Fortunately, many people who have fallen into crevasses have found something to hold onto and then climbed out.

People travelling across ice where there are crevasses use ropes to join themselves together. If a crevasse opens up and someone falls down it, the others in the group can pull them out.

Research stations

There are many research stations in both polar regions, ranging in size from a group of small huts, where a few scientists live, to the large underground research centre in the Antarctic, which is often home to over a thousand people. As well as studying the weather and the holes in the ozone layer, and the living things that are found in the polar regions, scientists in the Arctic are also studying:

1 how the Inuit survived in the past and whether their ways can help people today;

2 how the permafrost (see page 26) changes from year to year and how this change can affect wildlife;

3 the particles that cause the Aurora Borealis (see page 19) – because they affect electricity power lines and can cause blackouts and affect spacecraft such as **satellites**.

This scientist is studying a crevasse. It is about 20 metres deep.

In the Antarctic, scientists are also studying:

1 fossils in the rocks, to find out what life forms have lived in Antarctica in the past;

2 the rocks that make up the Antarctic continent, to find out how it formed;

3 rocks believed to be **meteorites**, which came from the Moon and Mars when they were struck by asteroids. These dark rocks are easy to see against the snow-white surface.

As both polar regions, but especially the Antarctic, have been little affected by humans, they are considered to be pure. International laws have been made to protect them from damage or pollution.

The tundra

The land around the Arctic Ocean is covered in ice and snow in the winter. When warmer weather returns, the snow and ice melt, revealing rocks, gravel and soil. About half a metre beneath the surface, the ground remains frozen. The frozen ground is called **permafrost**. The water that forms from the melted snow and ice cannot drain down through the permafrost, and so it collects into ponds and bogs. This whole area of land, underlaid with permafrost, is called the tundra.

Scientists visit the tundra to study the plants and animals that live there. They examine the life cycles of the wildlife and look at how different plants and animals manage to survive in the changing conditions.

The importance of soil

Water expands when it freezes. When ice forms in spaces in a rock, it pushes on the rock and breaks pieces off. Over thousands of years the freezing and thawing of ice on rocks has made large amounts of gravel and soil in the tundra. The soil provides a place where Arctic plants can sink their roots and hold on in the strong winds. Water collects in the soil and the plants use this to survive. The plants in turn provide food and shelter for animals, such as lemmings, ptarmigan and caribou.

Insect pests in the tundra

Many insects can survive through the winter in the tundra, as eggs or **pupa**. In summer, they turn into adults, which have wings, and fly about to find a mate. These insects need food to provide them with energy for flight, and many feed on blood.

Mosquitoes, midges and black flies form huge swarms when the air is still. The insects attack any bare skin they can find, to get a meal of blood. Mosquito bites can be painful. Travellers must use insect repellents on their skin to keep insects away. In some places they may need to wear head nets.

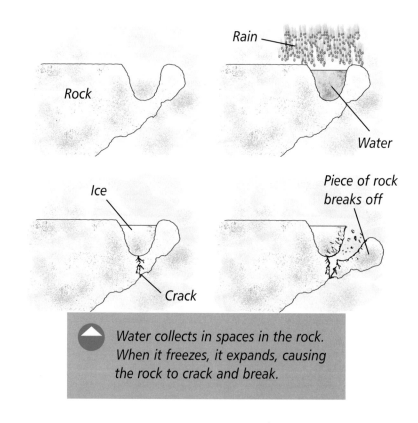

Rock

Rain

Water

Ice

Crack

Piece of rock breaks off

Water collects in spaces in the rock. When it freezes, it expands, causing the rock to crack and break.

How much does freezing affect rock?

To help them with their ideas, scientists sometimes copy in the laboratory what they have seen occurring naturally. You can copy a natural process – the weathering of rock – by using the kitchen as a laboratory. Make sure that the adults in your home or school agree.

You need two pieces of the same kind of rock (e.g. sandstone, chalk, limestone, or pumice stone) about 3 cm³, two tinfoil dishes, water, permission to use the freezer, magnifying glass.

1 Place one piece of rock in each dish.

2 Cover one of them with water.

3 Put both dishes in the freezer and leave them for a few hours or even a day.

4 Take the dishes out of the freezer and let the ice melt.

5 Pour out the water and look at the surfaces of the two rocks.

6 Rub your finger over the surfaces of the two rocks. You may find that pieces of grit fall off the rock that has been in the ice. Grit can form part of a soil.

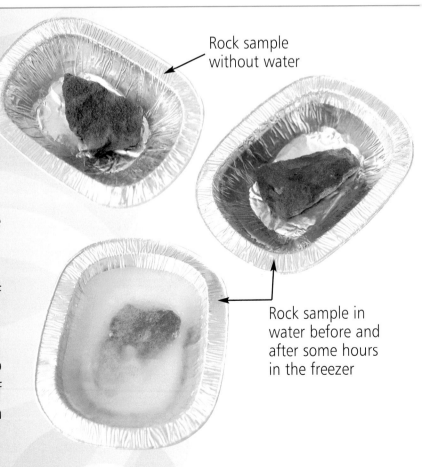

Rock sample without water

Rock sample in water before and after some hours in the freezer

Polar plants

You may think that no plants could survive in the snow and rocks of a polar landscape, but you would be wrong. Plants called **algae** are found worldwide. In polar regions some algae live in snow and rocks.

Algae

In the Antarctic, as summer begins, some banks of snow turn pink. If you looked at the snow under a microscope, you would find tiny pink algae. They live in the snow but, when the Sun returns to the sky, each one grows a tiny hair, which it uses to push itself up to near the snow surface. In this new position it can use the sunlight to make food to keep itself alive. It is thought that the chemical that makes the algae pink protects them from ultraviolet light (see page 11).

Even a bare sandstone rock may have algae living in it. Sandstone is made from grains of sand with gaps between them. The algae live in gaps near the surface, under grains that are **transparent**. Sunlight can pass through the transparent grains and, when some of it reaches the algae, it provides them with energy to make food.

Plants in the tundra

The soil of the tundra provides a place where plants can sink their roots and draw up the water and **minerals** they need. However, strong, cold, dry winds blow across the tundra and can quickly damage any plant that tries to grow high above the

The tundra provides food for some large animals, such as caribou.

soil. The plants that survive best keep close to the ground. Small plants such as the Arctic poppy thrive well, and even some trees, such as the dwarf willow, survive by growing their slender trunks along the ground.

Many tundra plants spend the winter as seeds. The warmth of summer makes the seeds sprout or **germinate**. The seedling, which grows out of the seed, quickly grows into a full-sized plant and makes flowers. These produce more seeds to survive in the following winter.

Does temperature affect germination?

Temperature affects the germination of all plants, not just those that grow in the tundra. See how temperature affects the germination of mustard seeds.

You need four pads of cotton wool about 8cm square, water, a measuring cylinder, mustard seeds, four polythene bags with seals, permission to use a fridge and a freezer.

1 Make each cotton wool pad wet by adding the same amount of water to each one.

2 Plant 10 mustard seeds on each pad.

3 Place each pad in a polythene bag and seal it.

4 Place one bag in the freezer, one in the fridge, one in a cold place such as a cupboard in the shade, and one in a warm place such as a sunny windowsill.

5 Check the bags every two days, for about two weeks, and look for signs of sprouting. Record your results each time you check the bags.

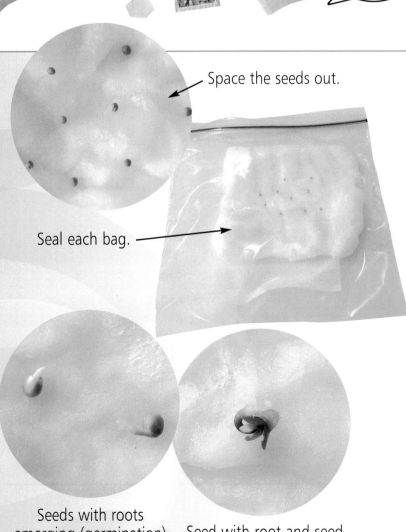

Space the seeds out.

Seal each bag.

Seeds with roots emerging (germination)

Seed with root and seed leaves emerging

Travelling in the polar regions

There is a variety of ways of travelling through the polar regions.

Walking in the tundra

In summer the land is cleared of snow, so strong boots are sufficient footwear. In some places paths have been made over many years, but where there are no paths, walkers must take extra care. On rocky ground there is a danger of twisting an ankle. In other places you may step into a bog.

Travelling over snow and ice

Skis allow a person to travel faster across snow and ice. In the polar regions skis are used for going up slopes as well as down. When used for climbing a slope, they must not be able to slide backwards.

Skis make it possible to travel where walking would be very hard.

Early travellers in the Arctic attached sealskin under part of their skis. The hairs in a seal's skin all point in one direction so that water flows over it easily while it is swimming. When the sealskin was attached to the skis, care was taken that the hairs pointed backwards. This meant that the hairs were flattened when the skis were going forwards and did not slow them down. But when the skier climbed uphill and the ski began to slide backwards, the hairs stuck out and stopped it doing so. The sticking out of the hairs increased the force called **friction** between the ski and the snow. Today, specially manufactured materials are stuck on the underside of skis, instead of sealskin.

Testing materials for sliding and gripping

Many carpets have fibres which all point in one direction, just like the hairs in a piece of sealskin. You can investigate how pieces of carpet slide down a slope and find the one that is best at sliding in one direction and gripping in the opposite direction.

You need a selection of types of carpet (each about 10cm square), a wooden plank with a shiny surface, a heavy wooden block, a ruler.

1 Study one carpet piece. Rub your hand over the fibres. You should find that they flatten together when you rub them in one direction. When rubbed in the opposite direction they separate and stick up a little.

Turn each carpet piece round, to test it a second time.

2 Place the carpet piece, fibres side down, on one end of the plank. Make sure that the fibres will flatten if you tip the plank.

Tip the plank to make a slope.

3 Start with the plank flat. Place the block on the carpet. Then tip the plank until the block and carpet start to slide. Measure and record the height of the end of the plank.

Measure this height.

4 Lower the plank and turn the carpet round so that the fibres will stick up when you tip the plank. Repeat step 3.

6 Find the smallest and greatest heights that you recorded. These tell you which carpet piece was best at sliding and gripping.

5 Repeat steps 2-4 with each carpet piece.

Snowshoes are made of light, bendy wood. They make walking over snow easier, by spreading the wearer's weight over a larger area than just the boots.

Snowshoes

Walking across powdery snow is a problem because you sink into the surface. If you just wear ordinary boots, all your weight pushes down through the small area of their heels and soles. This makes a high pressure on the snow and you sink in. If you wear snowshoes over your boots, as shown in the photograph, your weight is spread out over a wider area. This makes a lower pressure on the snow and you do not sink in so far.

Crampons

People who plan to walk across an icy surface fit crampons to the bottom of their boots. Crampons have sharp spikes which press down into the ice and provide grip. They let people walk without slipping and even give enough grip for a person to pull a sledge behind them.

Sledges

A sledge has two runners, which are made of metal or wood. As the lower surface of a runner touches the surface of the snow or ice, friction develops between them. A friction force stops one surface moving over the other, but its strength depends on the surfaces. If the surfaces are rough, the friction force is strong and a great deal of effort and energy are needed to pull one surface over the other. The runners of the sledge have very smooth surfaces, so that less effort and energy are needed to pull the sledge over the snow or ice.

Many people making an expedition in a polar region pull a sledge, carrying everything they need for their journey. The Inuit sometimes use a team of dogs called huskies to pull their sledges. In Lapland reindeer are sometimes used to pull sledges.

Snow machines

Vehicles are now widely used in polar regions. They are specially adapted to work in the low temperatures. Vehicles with engines and ordinary wheels cannot travel across polar regions because the wheels cannot grip the snow and ice. However, if a vehicle is fitted with caterpillar tracks, it can move over snow and ice and carry loads or pull sledges. A caterpillar track is a metal band that loops round the front and back wheels on each side of a vehicle.

The band has metal plates attached to it, and these have ridges across which bite into the snow and ice. When the front wheel turns, it pushes down a plate over which it can run. When the back wheel turns, it runs over a plate, then lifts it up and pushes it forwards to the front wheel. There may be other wheels between the front and back wheels to help the caterpillar track press close to the snow and ice.

Aircraft

Aeroplanes and helicopters fitted with skis are used to carry supplies and people quickly to the polar research stations. They are also used for rescue (see page 44).

In 1958 a team of scientists led by Edmund Hillary reached the South Pole in tractors fitted with caterpillar tracks.

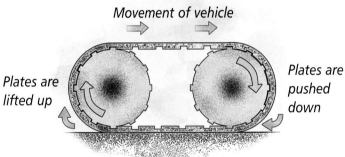

Movement of vehicle

Plates are lifted up

Plates are pushed down

Caterpillar tracks

Skidoos are small snow machines with just one caterpillar track and two skis, which act like runners on a sledge.

33

Finding the way

Sometimes it is difficult for people to find their way at the Poles. When low clouds cover the sky, light is reflected from them as well as from the snow. This makes shadows disappear and the horizon vanish. This is called a 'white-out'. Everything looks white and you cannot really see where you are going. People are in danger of walking off ice cliffs, because they cannot see the edge. When the clouds move away, the white-out disappears.

The effect of clear air

In many countries there are dust particles in the air, which make a haze. This helps us judge distances, because objects that are further away look less clear through the haze. In the polar regions, the air is very clear and there is no haze. This makes it difficult to judge distances, as everything can be seen clearly and it is hard to tell whether something is close or far away. One explorer thought he was looking at a mountain with two glaciers, on one side of an island. In fact he was looking at a walrus and the 'glaciers' were its tusks.

A GPS receiver enables people to find out their position.

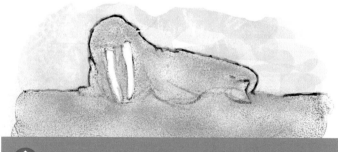

If you think this is something in the far distance, you may see it as an island with a mountain. If you know it is close, you will see it as a walrus.

Finding directions

Polar travellers use a compass and a **GPS** (global positioning system) receiver to help them find directions. GPS is a system of satellites which allows people to find their position anywhere on the Earth. The satellites constantly send out signals about their position. A person using GPS carries a receiver, about the size of a mobile phone. When it is switched on, it searches for signals from four of the satellites. The signals are sent into a computer in the receiver and the position of the person is shown on a screen. This can then be used with a map, to help the person plot their journey.

However, if polar travellers lose their compass and the batteries in their GPS receiver fail to work, they could still find north and south if they have a watch with hands.

Can you find north and south?

Many years ago it was discovered that the way the Sun moves regularly across the sky can be linked to the way the hour hand moves regularly across a watch face, to give the position of north and south. You can check how good this link is in the following activity.

You need a watch with hands, a compass, a sunny day.

In the Northern Hemisphere

1 Take off your watch and hold it in a horizontal position, so that the hour hand points towards the Sun. (NB In summer in the UK, you need to turn your watch back an hour to remove the effect of British Summer Time.)

2 Look at the position of the 12 mark on the watch face and make an angle in your mind between the hour hand and the 12 mark.

3 In your mind, draw a line **bisecting** the angle. This line gives the direction of north and south. The end of the line pointing away from the Sun is pointing north.

4 Check the directions you have found with a compass. How accurate is this way of finding north and south?

In the Southern Hemisphere

Follow the steps above, but place the 12 mark towards the Sun. The end of the line bisecting the angle and pointing away from the Sun is pointing south.

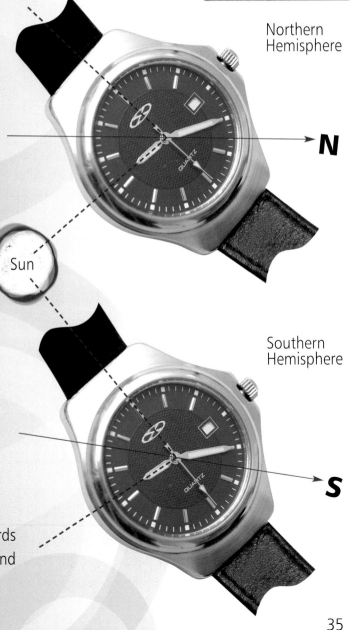

Northern Hemisphere

N

Sun

Southern Hemisphere

S

35

Shelter

Igloos are temporary shelters made from blocks of snow.

Many Arctic people live in modern houses today. The materials to make them are often brought in from other parts of the world. In the past, people used to live in simpler homes made from the materials that could be found in their surroundings.

Inuit homes

The Inuit survived by hunting, fishing and gathering berries. They needed to move around the Arctic for this, and built three types of home for different times of year.

The most famous polar shelter is the igloo. It was built by the Inuit and used as a temporary home while on a seal hunt in winter. An igloo is made from blocks of snow, which are cut with a toothed metal tool called a snow saw. The first blocks cut are arranged in a circle and the others are laid on top of them, like bricks in a wall. However, these blocks are tilted inwards. The blocks low down in the wall are only slightly tilted, but those high up may be almost horizontal as they make the igloo roof. The blocks are held together by knocking their edges together as they are placed in the wall.

For most of the winter the Inuit lived on the tundra, where they could find wood, stone and turf to use as building materials. They also used the bones of whales that they had caught. These materials were used to make houses with a large single room, similar to an igloo. In summer the Inuit lived in tents made from the skins of animals they caught for food.

Sami homes

The Sami also lived out in the tundra, with their reindeer herds, in the summer. At this time they lived in large cone-shaped tents called teepees, made from wooden poles and reindeer skins. In winter they lived further south in wooden huts.

Scientists working in polar regions live in research stations (see page 25).

Fire

In summer on the tundra there is plenty of wood to make a fire, but in winter this is covered up. In the past, the Inuit managed to make a fire in their igloos by carrying with them the materials and equipment they needed. They set out a stone or metal tray called a koodlik and put some seal blubber in it. (Blubber is a fatty substance that seals make under their skin. It insulates them, keeping them warm.) Next, the Inuit set out some **tinder** made from small dry plants such as moss. A flint and steel were then struck together close to the tinder.

The striking of the flint and steel produced sparks and some fell on the tinder. The heat from the sparks made the tinder start to burn. The flames from the burning tinder were used to melt the blubber and make it catch fire. The heat from the burning blubber was used to keep the people in the igloo warm and to dry their clothes, to melt ice for water and to cook food.

The snow blocks of an igloo contain air, which acts as an insulator. This stops the heat passing through the blocks and melting them. The insulating property of the blocks also helps to keep the inside of the igloo warm.

On expeditions, people use stoves which burn fuels such as methylated spirits or petrol. The stoves are lit with matches.

When fires are used in shelters such as igloos, and stoves are used in tents, there must be ventilation to remove carbon monoxide, a poisonous gas that is made when materials burn.

This Sami family have gathered around their fire to eat and talk.

Food

The food that we eat over the course of a week or a month is called our diet. A diet can contain vegetables, meat, fish, fruit and dairy products, such as cheese and milk. These foods contain nutrients, which are substances that our body needs to keep healthy.

- Proteins are nutrients found in meat and beans. They help us to grow, and repair cuts and bruises.

- Carbohydrates are nutrients found in bread and pasta. They provide the body with energy.

- Fats are nutrients found in cheese and chocolate. They can supply even larger amounts of energy than carbohydrates.

Some Arctic peoples still live so far from towns today that they must hunt for food as their ancestors did. This woman is scraping blubber from sealskin to make a meal rich in fat.

Energy needs

Energy is needed by all living things, simply to keep them alive. It has many forms and can change from one form to another. For example, plants change some of the energy in sunlight into chemical energy, which is stored as food. When we eat food, we change some of the chemical energy into heat energy, to warm our body, and into movement energy, to give us the power to walk about.

People who live in the polar regions and people on expeditions there need large amounts of energy to keep them warm. If they are clambering over glaciers and pulling sledges, they need large amounts of energy to move, too. Fats can provide them with the energy they need. People in polar regions need a diet with much more fat in it than people who live in warmer places and do not take so much exercise.

In the past, when most Inuit hunted for food, they got their fat from seal and whale blubber. Now they get the fat they need from the same foods as people on expeditions – foods such as butter, cheese, chocolate and nuts.

Testing foods for fat

A simple way of testing a food for fat is to rub it on a piece of paper, let the paper dry, then hold it up to the light. If you can see light through the paper (i.e. the paper has become **translucent**), the food contains fat.

You need white paper, a stop clock, a selection of foods such as cheese, butter, chocolate, carrot, potato.

Warning!
Do not use nuts if you are allergic to them.

1 Take one of the foods and rub it backwards and forwards across a piece of paper for 5 seconds.

2 Write the name of the food on the paper. Then leave the paper to dry.

3 Repeat steps 1 and 2 with all the foods.

4 Hold each paper in turn up to the light and look for a translucent 'window' in it. If there is one, it has been made by fat in the food.

5 Sort the foods into those that would be useful for supplying energy on an expedition and those that would not be useful for supplying energy.

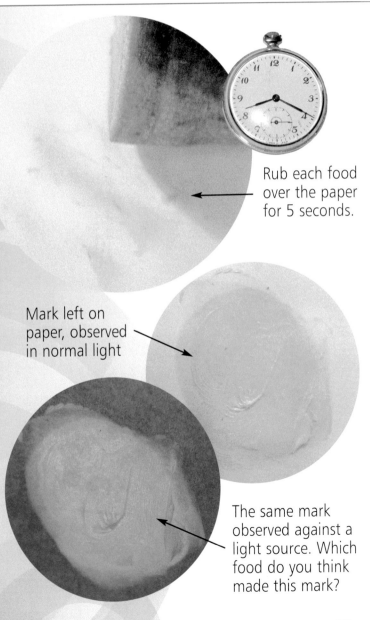

Rub each food over the paper for 5 seconds.

Mark left on paper, observed in normal light

The same mark observed against a light source. Which food do you think made this mark?

Water

There is more water in the polar regions than in many other places on the Earth. In winter, however, none of it is in liquid form that can be drunk. It is in the form of snow and ice.

You may think that a simple way to take in the water would be to put ice or snow in your hands or your mouth, let it melt and then drink it. But this should not be done, because it would cause you to lose vital body heat and it may also damage your mouth and lips.

Turning snow to water

If wood can be found to light a fire, a lump of snow may be placed on a pole and pointed towards the fire like a huge marshmallow. As the heat melts the snow, the water can drip into a can by the fire. The melted snow can then be drunk.

Sea ice and freshwater ice

There are two kinds of ice – sea ice and freshwater ice. Sea ice is made from seawater and contains large amounts of salt. Sea ice cannot be used to make a drink because the salt in it can fatally damage many organs inside the body. Freshwater ice made from snow is safe to melt and make into a drink. Sea ice can be recognized by its white appearance, while freshwater ice is blue.

Water in the tundra

In summer, water can be taken from ponds in the tundra. It must be boiled for at least ten minutes, to kill any germs that may be present. Then it can be cooled and used as a drink.

A lump of snow can be melted to make drinking water.

Polar animals

Arctic animals

In winter most of the land is covered in snow, yet some large animals still manage to survive there. Reindeer, caribou and musk ox scrape away the snow with their hooves, to get at the tundra plants growing underneath. Other large animals living in the Arctic include the wolf and the polar bear.

In the summer many small animals such as lemmings, shrews and squirrels can also be seen. In winter they live in tunnels under the snow, or make nests and hibernate.

Beware of bears

A hungry polar bear can attack and eat people, if given a chance. People on expeditions in polar bear country can set up trip wires around their camp. If a polar bear comes to investigate the camp in the night, it will stumble into the trip wire. The movement of the wire operates a switch, which sets off a thunder flash. The loud sound and light frighten the bear away and also wake up the people and make them aware of the danger.

Polar bears are some of the largest carnivores on Earth.

People on expeditions in the tundra in the summer may find that brown bears are present too. Bears have a good sense of smell and often search for an easy meal, such as the food at a camp. After a meal, campers should tidy away the food scraps and store all food at least 100 metres away from the tents. If food is stored in a tent, a bear may pay it a visit.

Antarctic animals

Most of the Antarctic continent is covered in snow and ice. In some places there are dry rocky valleys, but there is nowhere where enough plants grow for animals such as reindeer to feed on. The only animals found on the land are penguins and seals and they get their food from the sea, in the form of fish. Most penguins stay at the coast, but the largest kind, the emperor penguin, moves inland to breed in the winter.

Emperor penguins are over 1 metre tall. They can dive to depths of over 250 metres.

1 cubic centimetre

Surface area of each side is 1 square centimetre.

4 cubic centimetres

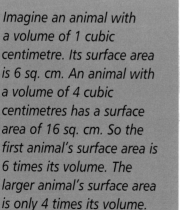

Imagine an animal with a volume of 1 cubic centimetre. Its surface area is 6 sq. cm. An animal with a volume of 4 cubic centimetres has a surface area of 16 sq. cm. So the first animal's surface area is 6 times its volume. The larger animal's surface area is only 4 times its volume.

Size and survival

An animal gets heat energy from its food and loses some of the heat through its body surface. The diagrams show that a small animal has a large surface area compared to its body volume. A larger animal has a smaller surface compared to its volume.

Small animals have a small volume to produce heat and a large area to lose it from. Larger animals have a large volume to produce heat, but a comparatively smaller surface area to lose it from. This explains why larger animals, like the musk ox, lose heat more slowly than smaller ones, like the shrew. The larger animals can survive in cold conditions, while smaller ones must shelter in burrows under the snow. The snow acts as a blanket to keep the animals warm.

Musk ox

Shrew

Comparing how large and small animals lose heat

In this activity you use model animals made from pans, to compare how they lose heat.

1 After reading 'Size and survival' on page 42, make a prediction about which of the two pans will lose heat more slowly.

2 Three-quarters fill each pan with warm water. (Ask an adult to help you.)

3 Place the thermometer in the water of the small pan so that the bulb is in the centre of the water. This measures the 'core temperature' of the body. Write down the temperature.

4 Repeat step 3 with the larger pan.

5 Repeat steps 3 and 4 every two minutes for 40 minutes.

6 Compare the way that the 'core temperatures' fell. Do the results match your prediction?

Take the temperature of each pan every two minutes over a 40-minute period.

Rescue

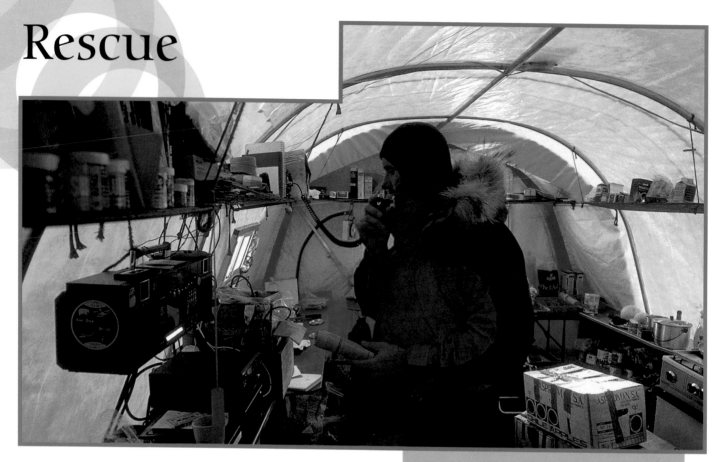

 Scientists on polar expeditions have radios or phones to communicate with the research base.

People setting out on a polar expedition must take everything they will need with them, because there is often little chance of finding things like wood or food along the way. They take a medical kit, and one of the expedition team may be a doctor or have medical training. Meals are worked out beforehand, and the food is stored on the sledges. Tents, cooking gear, spare clothes and even a needle and thread are taken along.

Even with all this preparation, things can go wrong and the team may need to be rescued. For example, someone may be injured when they fall down a crevasse or someone may suffer so much from frostbite that they need hospital treatment. The weather may be so severe that the team have to rest in their tents for many days. This unexpected stop can mean that the food supply runs out before the end of the journey.

People on expeditions may have a satellite phone, which they can use to contact a rescue base. They may also have a rescue beacon, which sends a signal to a rescue base. The rescuers may have to travel hundreds of kilometres, through dangerous conditions, either by aeroplane, which has skis for landing in ice and snow, or by snowmobile.

Sending signals – Morse code

Phones and beacons may sometimes fail, so it is useful to know other ways of signalling for help. For many years the Morse code was used to send messages. Here are some letters of the code:

A · –   R · – ·   T –
K – · –   S · · ·   0 – – –

Sending messages by light

Imagine that you are stranded on a block of ice called an ice floe, which has broken off from an ice sheet. The floe is slowly moving out into the Arctic Ocean. It is the end of summer and the days are becoming dark. You see a ship in the distance. Can you make a circuit and send signals to save your life? Can a person on the ship signal back?

You need two 1.5V batteries, two switches, two 3V light bulbs, six wires, a friend to work the second circuit.

1 Make two circuits as shown in the photograph. Set them up at opposite ends of a room.

2 Work one circuit yourself while your friend works the other. Use the letters of Morse code on page 44 to send each other the following messages. A dot is a short flash and a dash is a longer flash.

AAAAA. It means 'I have a message.'
TTTTT. It means 'I am receiving you.'
SOS. It means 'Save our souls', which means 'Help'.
R. It means 'Message received.'
AR. It means 'End of message.'

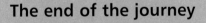

The end of the journey

When people reach the end of a journey, they usually feel they have learnt a lot along the way. How did you get on on your journey through the polar regions? Can you name two groups of people who live in the Arctic? Can you explain why it is so cold at the Poles? Where would you find permafrost? Also during the journey you have had chances to try out your science skills of observing, predicting and experimenting. What did you discover? Although most of us live far from the Poles, the conditions there can affect us. If you get frost and snow in the winter where you live, it may be caused by cold air that has travelled from the polar region nearest you.

Glossary

albedo — the power of a surface to reflect the light and heat it receives from a source such as the Sun.

algae — tiny plant-like living things that can only be seen clearly with a microscope.

Antarctic Circle — an imaginary line around the Earth, between the South Pole and the equator. It is found on a map at the parallel of latitude 66°32′ S.

Arctic Circle — an imaginary line around the Earth, between the equator and the North Pole. It is found on a map at the parallel of latitude 66°32′ N.

axis — an imaginary line running through the centre of the Earth, from the North Pole to the South Pole.

balaclava — a piece of clothing made of wool which fits tightly over the head but leaves parts of the face uncovered.

beacon — a light set up to guide people to it.

bisect — divide something into two equal parts.

CFCs — chlorofluorocarbons. These are chemicals which have been used in aerosol sprays, in cooling systems for refrigerators, and for making foam plastics.

condense — change from a gas to a liquid.

conductor — a substance which allows heat or electricity to pass through it easily.

constellation — a group of stars which people in the past believed made the shape of a person, animal or object.

crevasses — very deep openings in glaciers.

density — a measure of the way the particles in a substance are packed together.

expedition — a journey made for a particular purpose, such as to find out about the plants and animals in a place.

firn — a material made from snowflakes that have been squashed together but still have air spaces between them.

friction — a force that is produced when two surfaces rub together.

germinate — send out a root to collect water and a shoot to make food. This is the action of the tiny plant inside a seed as the seed coat breaks open.

glaciers — very large bodies of ice which move slowly down valleys.

GPS — global positioning system. In this system, satellites and a small computer in a receiver are used to show the position of a person or an object on the Earth.

ice cap	a huge body of ice which covers a large area of land and does not melt away in summer.	**pupa**	the stage in the life of some insects in which they change from a larva into an adult.
ice shelf	a huge piece of ice made by ice from an ice cap that has moved slowly into the sea.	**reflected**	made to change direction when hitting a surface.
insulating	stopping the movement of heat, or stopping the movement of electricity.	**research station**	a building or group of buildings in which scientists live and work.
lenses	discs of glass or plastic. In sunglasses, a dark material is added to them to stop some light from passing through.	**satellite**	an object which moves in an orbit around the Earth, carrying a range of electrical devices, such as computers, radio transmitters and receivers.
lichens	plants formed by types of fungi and algae living together.	**tinder**	dry material, such as grass, which can be used to start a fire.
meteorites	pieces of rock from space that have fallen onto the surface of the Earth.	**translucent**	describes a material that lets some light pass through it. Things cannot be seen clearly through the material.
minerals	substances in the soil that a plant needs for good health. The minerals dissolve in water in the soil and are taken into the plant by the roots.	**transparent**	describes a material that allows large amounts of light to pass through it. Things can be seen clearly through it.
observation	looking at the way something is, or the way in which something happens.	**tundra**	the land in the Arctic that has permafrost beneath its surface in summer.
orbit	the curved path of a planet around the Sun, or of a moon around a planet, or of a satellite around a planet, moon, or the Sun.	**ultraviolet**	a form of energy. It travels as waves across space and through the air. It has a shorter wavelength than light and cannot be detected by our eyes.
permafrost	the part of the soil in a polar region which remains frozen all year.	**water vapour**	a gas which water forms when it evaporates.

Index

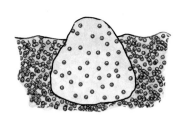

© 2004 White-Thomson Publishing Ltd

White-Thomson Publishing Ltd,
2-3 St Andrew's Place, Lewes,
East Sussex BN7 1UP

Published in Great Britain in 2004 by Hodder
Wayland

This paperback edition published in 2007 by Wayland
Reprinted in 2008

This book was produced for White-Thomson
Publishing Ltd by Ruth Nason.

Design and illustration: Carole Binding

The right of Peter D. Riley to be identified as
the author of this work has been asserted by
him in accordance with the Copyright,
Designs and Patents Act 1988.

British Library Cataloguing in Publication Data
Riley, Peter D.
    In Polar Regions. - (Survivor's Science)
    1. Polar regions - Juvenile literature
    2. Tundra ecology - Juvenile literature
    3. Snow ecology - Juvenile literature
    I. Title
    577.5'86
ISBN 978 0 7502 4536 4

Printed in China

Wayland
338 Euston Road, London NW1 3BH

Wayland is an imprint
of Hachette Children's Books,
an Hachette Livre UK Company.
www.hachettelivre.co.uk

Acknowledgements
The author and publishers thank the following for their permission to reproduce photographs: Corbis: pages 6 and 33 (Staffan Widstrand), 17 (Kennan Ward), 32 (Carl & Ann Purcell), 34 (Caroline Penn), 44 (Morton Beebe); Ecoscene: pages 11 (Graham Neden), 30 (Graham Neden); Science Photo Library: pages 4 (British Antarctic Survey), 8 (CNES, 1994 Distribution Spot Image), 10 (Simon Fraser), 12 (David Vaughan), 23 (Bernhard Edmaier), 25 (David Vaughan); Still Pictures: pages 7 and 42 (Joel Bennett), 15 (Michael Sewell), 18 (Clyde H. Smith), 19 (Rosing-UNEP), 20 (Klaus Andrews), 22 (B. & C. Alexander), 24 and cover (Emmanuel Jeanjean), 28 (J. J. Alcalay), 36 (Robert Schoen), 37 (Pal Hermansen), 38 and cover (J. P. Sylvestre), 41 and 1 (Thomas D. Mangelsen). The illustration on page 14 was drawn, with permission, from a photograph by Robert Weight/Ecoscene. The science activity photographs are by Carole Binding.

Surviv...

Po... ...ions

...eter D. Riley

WAYLAND